Check Up Tests in Workskills

Redvers Brandling

M
Macmillan Education

To the pupil

In each test there are some questions which you must answer with full sentences and some which need only short answers. Read each question very carefully and make sure you understand what is needed. Then answer the questions exactly as you are told. It is important to number each part of your answer correctly.

If you get stuck on one part of a question, don't waste time on it but carry on with the next ones. You can always come back to it when you have finished the rest of the test.

Remember that we can learn from our mistakes, so if you get a wrong answer, try and learn why you went wrong, and make sure you get it right next time.

Test 1

1. The index of a book tells you on what pages in the book you can find more information about the subjects mentioned. For example, in a geography book if you saw in the index:

   Bombay 43
   Dunedin 79

   you would know that for information about these cities you would turn to the page numbers shown.
   Look at this section of an index from an international cookery book:

   bamboo shoots 23   dahl   30
   banana fritters 25   gazpacho 29
   boxty   57   kebab   45
   colcannon   73   kedgeree 47
   corn chowder   46   latkes   51
   curry powder   80   macaroni 55
   curry, vegetable 39

   Now write down the pages you would look at if you wanted to find answers to the following questions.

   a) How many potatoes are used in boxty?
   b) Is colcannon a hot meal?
   c) Are Jewish potato cakes called latkes?
   d) How should you serve gazpacho soup?
   e) Do you use eggs in making banana fritters?
   f) What is curry powder made from?
   g) Does kebab or kedgeree take the longest time to make?
   h) How much onion do you need in corn chowder?
   i) Is dahl an Indian dish?
   j) Can macaroni be served with a milk pudding?

2. The picture shows a wall with three openings in it.

   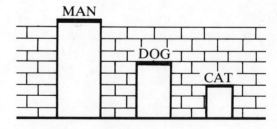

   Answer each of the following questions in a sentence.
   a) Through which openings could the man, dog and cat all pass?
   b) Only one of these living creatures could pass through all openings. Which one is this?
   c) Why are two of the openings really unnecessary?

3. Most clothes we buy have labels on them to help us look after them properly. Some of these labels are:

Meaning: Do not iron   Hand wash only   Do not dry clean   Can be dry cleaned   Can be tumble dried

Draw the signs you would find on.

   a) a shirt which could not be ironed
   b) a coat that could be dry cleaned
   c) a dress that could be tumble dried
   d) a pullover that could only be washed by hand
   e) a coat that could not be ironed or dry cleaned

4. Look at this picture:

Now choose the sentence in each section which best fits the picture.

   a) The man will fall on land.   The man will fall in water.   The man will jump to safety.
   b) He was going for a swim.   He jumped in.   He is the victim of an accident.
   c) He was dressed for swimming.   He was not dressed for swimming.   He has changed to swim.
   d) Something unexpected has happened.   Nothing unexpected has happened.   Everything is fine.
   e) He wants to put the case in the water.   He brought the case for swimming.   He just happened to by carrying the case.

5. Read this passage carefully:
   'Vincent's plane landed at the airport in Jamaica. He was glad to be home again. He had changed out of his thick pullover on the flight over. The Customs Officer soon checked his baggage. He admired Vincent's camera.'

   Answer the following questions in sentences.

   a) How had Vincent been travelling?
   b) Where is his home?
   c) Had he come from a warmer or colder place?
   d) Give one reason why you can tell he had come from another country.
   e) Had he any baggage with him?
   f) Why is it likely Vincent had taken some photographs?
   g) Why would Vincent be familiar with Jamaica?

Test 2

1.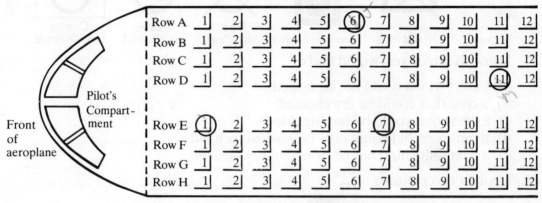

   This diagram shows the seating plan in an aeroplane. To find your seat you need to know two facts: the row you are in (A, B, C, etc.) and your seat number (1, 2, 3, etc). So, if your seat was A1 you would have a window seat in the front row.

   A family travelling on this plane could only get 4 separate seats, They are marked on the seating plan with a ring round each.

   a) Two members of the family were in the same row. What were their seat numbers in this row?
   b) John was the only one of the family to have a seat beside a window. In which seat was he sitting?
   c) Mary was sitting farthest from the pilot's compartment. What row was her seat in?
   d) If we now know where John and Mary sat, and Mr Jones' seat was E1, what was Mrs Jones' seat?
   e) If Mary moved one seat forward in the same row, towards the pilot's compartment, what would be her new seat?
   f) Which member of the family is nearest to seat A5?

2. Write down in your book what has been missed out of each of the following.

   Here is an example to help you: 2, 4, 6, –, 10, 12, 14, –, 18.
   Answer = 8 and 16.

   a) ABC–EFG–IJ   b) ×□○, □___○, ×○___   c) 4__12 16__24

   d) ▲△△, △▲__, △▲__   e) he, him, his, she, –, hers, –, them, theirs

   f) ½, ½, –, ⅓, ⅓, ¼, ¼, ¼, –.   g) BOMBAY   B–MBAY   BO--A-

3.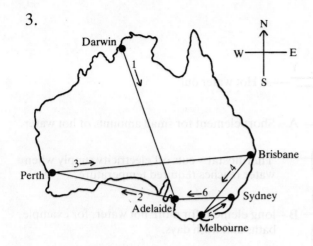

Look at this map. It shows the flight plan of a Quantas jet. Answer the following questions in sentences.

a) Where is the first stop after leaving Darwin?
b) Which is the last stop?
c) Which is the shortest flight?
d) On which route does the jet fly over the sea?
e) What is the destination of route 5?
f) Which town is on the west coast?
g) Which town is farthest north?

4.
> **TONGUE TIED?   NOT SURE WHAT TO SAY?**
>
> *DON'T WORRY!*
>
> **TAKE A COURSE OF "LO-KWAYSHUS" THE NEW TALKING PILLS!**
>
> Take thrice daily at regular intervals, preferably after meals so that you don't talk with your mouth full.
>
> Get a week's supply NOW!

Answer each of the following questions in a sentence.

a) How many exclamation marks does this advertisement use?
b) How many pills a day does it recommend?
c) According to the advertisement would taking pills at 9am, 10pm and 11pm in one day be the best dose?
d) How many pills does the advertisement suggest you buy NOW!
e) Should you take the pill before or after lunch?

5. For each of the following statements write down 'F' if you think it is a *fact*, or 'O' if you think it is an *opinion*.

a) 2+2=4
b) Africa is a continent.
c) He should do well in the test.
d) May is the fifth month of the year.
e) Summer could be hot this year.
f) I-N-D-I-A spells India.
g) Telephone numbers are found in a directory.

Test 3

1.

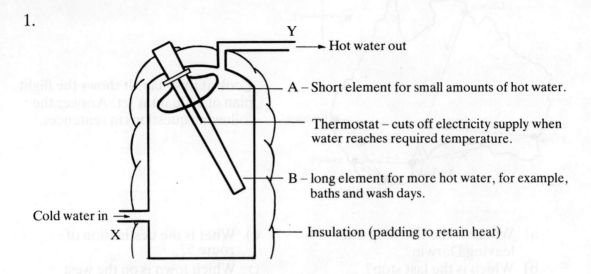

This is a diagram of an immersion heater. It is a tank of water which is always kept full. The water in it is heated by two elements (A and B). Each element has a separate switch.

Answer each of the following questions in a sentence.

a) Where does the cold water go into the tank?
b) What is the insulation for?
c) Which element would you switch on to give you enough hot water to wash your hands?
d) Which part of the tank's water would get hot first if you switched on both elements?
e) What is the name of the piece of equipment which cuts off the electricity supply when the water is hot enough?
f) From which point does the hot water leave the tank?
g) What would happen to the water in the tank if the electricity was not switched on?
h) When will cold water enter the tank?

2.

a) Re-arrange the numbers of the above pictures so that they show the right order for the things happening.

b) The following sentences have been written down in the wrong order. Re-write them in what you think is the right order:
He let it off the leash.   John decided to take his dog for a walk.   The dog ran away.

c) 2, 4, 6, 8, 10, 12 is correct but 9, 6, 3, 18, 15, 12 is not correct. Write out the second set of figures so that they are correct.

3. Look at the words which have been underlined in these two examples:
hot   warm   <u>boiling</u>   cold   <u>freezing</u>   cool

Using this information to help you, write out the words which you think should be underlined in the following:

a) large   big   enormous
b) small   microscopic   little
c) loud   noisy   deafening
d) feast   dinner   lunch
e) valuable   priceless   precious
f) speaking   shouting   talking
g) wind   breeze   hurricane

4. Look at this diagram showing children and their pets.

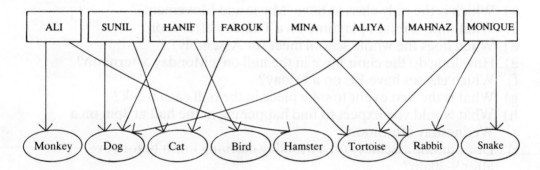

Now answer the following questions as briefly as you can.
a) Which child has no pets?
b) Which is the most popular pet?
c) How many pets have Sunil, Hanif and Aliya between them?
e) Apart from Ali, how many other people have two pets?
f) Who has most pets?
g) Which four are the least common pets?
h) Which child has a dog and a bird?
i) Who owns a snake?
j) Name all the children who own either a dog or cat or both.

5. Write out the following sentences, filling in each gap with the right word:
a) A book of maps is called an a_____.
b) You can look up the meaning of words in a d_____.
c) Telephone numbers are listed in a d_____.
d) Arrival and departure times are given in a t_____.

9

Test 4

	MONDAY	TUESDAY	WEDNESDAY	THURSDAY	FRIDAY
9am	ASSEMBLY 9am Junior 9-30am Infant	ASSEMBLY 9 am Junior 9-30am Class 2 Music	ASSEMBLY 9am Whole School 9-45am Class 2 PE	ASSEMBLY 9am Junior 9-30am Hymn Practice	ASSEMBLY 9am Junior 9-30am Infant Music
	INFANT PLAYTIME 10-25 – 11-40am JUNIORS 10-40 – 10-55am					
		ASSEMBLY 10-40am Infant 11-30am Class 3 PE	10-40am Class 8 PE 11-20am Class 7 PE	ASSEMBLY 10-40am Infant	11am Class 1 PE 11-30am Class 2 PE
12 – 1-30 pm	LUNCH JUNIORS 12 – 12-40pm INFANTS 12-40 – 1.30pm				
	1-30pm Instrumental Music Group	1-30pm Class 4 PE	1-30pm Class 9 PE 2pm Class 10 PE	1-30pm Class 5 PE	1-30pm Class 6 PE 2pm Class 9 Music Movement
	JUNIOR PLAYTIME 2-10 – 2.25pm INFANTS 2-25 – 2-40pm				
3-30 pm	2-25 Choir	Indoor Games Classes 5 and 6	Indoor Games Classes 1 and 2	Indoor Games Classes 3 and 4	ASSEMBLY 3pm Infant

1. The diagram above shows the hall timetable for a Junior and Infant school. Answer the following questions as briefly as possible.

    a) Which is the only day to have a blank period?
    b) Which is the only class to have 'Music and Movement'?
    c) What time is infant playtime on a Tuesday afternoon?
    d) When does the whole school meet for Assembly?
    e) How long do the choir have in the hall on a Monday afternoon?
    f) Which classes have PE on a Friday?
    g) What is the first event to take place in the hall each week?
    h) What would you expect to find happening in the hall at 3pm on a Wednesday afternoon?
    i) Does junior assembly on a Monday morning finish before or after 9-30am?
    j) Only one class immediately follows an infant assembly with PE. Which is it?

2. Write, or draw, in your books what should come next in each of the following:

    a) A C E G ?   b) 👆 👆 ?

    c) SINGAPORE, SINGAPOR, SINGAPO, ?   d) ?——E2 (N1/S3)

3. Write in your book the word which is out of alphabetical order in each of the following:

    a) crate   crave   crawl   crayfish   crank
    b) leap   leave   lease   least   leather
    c) pyramid   pygmy   pyjamas   pylon
    d) street   straw   stray   streak   stream
    e) skill   skin   skimp   stray   skirt
    f) pearl   peat   peasant   pebble   peek

4. These advertisements appeared in a local paper:

PETS AND LIVESTOCK

ONE YEAR OLD pedigree goat. £25 o.n.o. Ring 2457.
Ref. OM14

CAVALIER King Charles spaniel (dog), good pedigree. Kennel club registered. 3 mths old. £75. Ring 2331 after 6pm.
Ref. OM27

PROFESSIONAL CLIPPING and grooming. All breeds, speciality poodles. Will collect and deliver. Tel. 3664.
Ref. OM 36.

OLDER TYPE Upright Piano. Nice condition. Ideal for learner. £65. Ring 5502.
Ref. LX25

Answer each of the following questions in a sentence.

a) What is the reference number for the advertisement which has obviously got into the wrong section?
b) Would you telephone about the spaniel for sale at 2-30pm?
c) Which is the only advertisement to offer a service?
d) How many of the animals mentioned are pedigrees?
e) Write down all the dogs which are mentioned by breed.
f) What would you be enquiring about if you rang 5502?
g) Which is older, the goat or the spaniel?
h) Only one advertisement mentions no prices, Which is it?

5. Look at these cards.

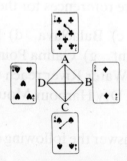

a) If each person changed his card with the person opposite, what card would C have?
b) If A and C changed cards, and A then gave his card to the person on his right, what card would D have?
c) If D gave his card to the person on his left and then received the card from the person opposite, what card would D now have?
d) If everybody passed their cards round once in a clockwise move what card would C then have?

Test 5

Map of Jamaica

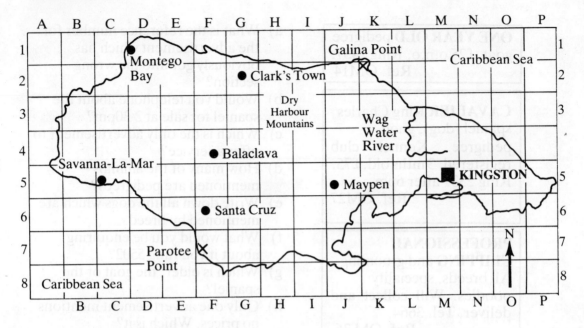

1. Look at this map of Jamaica. Find Maypen. If you look at the top (or bottom) of the map you will see that Maypen is in the row of squares marked by the letter J. If you look along from the side of the map you will see that Maypen is in the row of squares numbered 5.
   We can say then that Maypen is in Square J5 on the map.

   Now write in your book the square references for the following:

   a) Montego Bay   b) Kingston   c) Balaclava   d) Savanna-la-Mar
   e) Clark's Town   f) Parotee Point   g) Galina Point   h) Santa Cruz
   i) In which square does the Wag Water River reach the sea?
   j) Over which two squares do the Dry Harbour Mountains stretch?

2. Look at the map again and then answer the following questions in sentences.

   a) Name the only mountain range shown.   b) Which is the biggest town shown?
   c) Which is the most northerly of the 'points' shown?
   d) Which four inland towns are shown?   e) Which sea surrounds the coast of Jamaica?
   f) On which coast does the Wag Water River enter the sea? – North, South, East or West?

12

3.

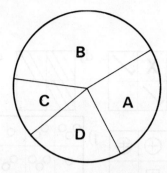

This chart shows the favourite drinks of a group of forty-eight children. Look at the following:

    A   –   Cocoa   –   10 children
    ?   –   Milk   –   20 children
    C   –   Coffee   –   ? children
    D   –   Tea   –   12 children

Answer the following questions with either a word, a letter or a number only.

a) What letter in the chart stands for milk?
b) How many children like coffee?
c) Which letter shows the drink 10 children like?
d) Which letter shows how many children like tea?
e) How many children altogether like milk or tea best?

4. Sort out the following words into alphabetical order. Put in capital letters where they are needed.
yacht   ugly   valerie   tent   xylophone   zena
wilson   yugoslavia

5. If a train pulled out of the station at 18.15 hours the hands on the station clock would look like this:

Draw diagrams to show what they would look like at:

a) 15.00 hours   b) 08.30 hours   c) 12.00 hours   d) 19.45 hours
e) 00.15 hours

Test 6

1. a) [XX / X_] b) [OX / _O] c) [X✓ / _✓] d) [hatched / _] e) [F ⊓ / _ ⊥] f) [人 人 / 人 _]
   g) [+ ++ / ++ _] h) [. ⊚ / ⊚ _] i) [⊕ ⊕ / ⊞ _] j) [grid with circles]

   Copy the puzzles above into your book and complete the empty square in each case.

2. Look at the pictures below and the three descriptions beside each. Choose the best description in each case and write it out in full.

   a) a man
   a man with legs
   a man with a sword

   b) a foot with a shoe on it
   a foot with a high heeled shoe on it
   a shoe

   c) a man with one eye
   a young man
   a man with a patch over one eye

   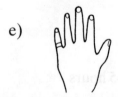
   d) a race
   a hundred metre race
   three people running

   e) a hand
   a right hand with a ring on
   a left hand with a ring on the little finger

3. Inside the brackets of the following words is a letter which completes the first word, and begins the second.
   Example: TEN (T) IN gives the two words TENT and TIN

   Work out what the missing letter is in the following, and write down the two words for each.

   a) PI (?) GG   b) TO (?) ELLOW   c) DO (?) ORILLA
   d) FRIEN (?) OCTOR

4. Here are the 26 letters of the alphabet:

   A B C D E F G H I J K L M N O P Q R S T U V W X Y Z

   Write down the letters required to answer the following questions.

   a) What is the tenth letter of the alphabet?
   b) Which letter is third from the end of the alphabet?
   c) Which letter is exactly half way between J and N?
   d) If the alphabet was written backwards which would be the last letter?
   e) Which two letters are used most in the word SHEERNESS?
   f) Look at this word: JOYFUL. Which of its letters is nearest the end of the alphabet?
   g) If the last ten letters were removed from the alphabet which letter would then be last?

5. Look at this diagram:

   Numbers of Thousands living there

	1	2	3	4	5	6	7	8
Tanjong Pagar Road								
Keppel Road								
Gelang Road								
Tanjong Rhu Road								
Shenton Way								

   This diagram shows that these roads had a certain number of people living in them. These numbers were:

   Tanjong Pagar – 2,500; Keppel – 4,000; Gelang – 3,000;
   Tanjong Rhu – 4,900; Shenton – 700.

   Now draw a similar diagram to show the following information:
   Serangoon Road – 5,000 people; Kampong Java Road – 7,000;
   Leng Kee Road – 800; Tiong Bahru Road – 5,900;
   Pasir Panjang Road – 6,500.

6. Copy out the passage below, filling in the gaps with the correct words from the list below:

   In order to send a letter you must put it in an _____ .
   On this you should write the name and _____ of the person you are sending it to. To pay for delivering it, you must fix on a _____, which is cancelled out by a _____ so that it cannot be used again. This will show the _____ as well as the place where the letter was posted.

   number   address   parcel   envelope   stamp
   postman   date   postmark

15

Test 7

1. The Beaufort notation is a type of code which tells us what the weather is like. Here are some examples of this code:

   b – blue sky (not more than ¼ cloud);
   bc – (sky ½ covered with cloud);
   c – cloudy; d – drizzle;
   f – fog (visibility between 200-1000 metres);
   F – thick fog (visibility less than 200 metres);
   L – Lightning;
   r – rain;
   rr – continuous rain;
   R – heavy rain.

   Now write down the letter (or letters) of the code which you would use to describe the following weather conditions.

   a) The sky was half blue and half cloudy.
   b) It was drizzling.
   c) It rained all day without stopping.
   d) The rain was extremely heavy.
   e) The fog was so thick that drivers could only see 50 metres.
   f) It was a cloudy day.
   g) It was raining and there was lightning.
   h) There was not a cloud in the sky.

2. You would probably be surprised at how many people are called 'Christmas.' Look at these details from a telephone directory.

Christmas, A.,	3 Walter Ave.,	N.17.	01 369 0122
Christmas, A.B.,	14 Sigmund Street,	N.20.	01 452 3853
Christmas, F.,	6 Albert Square,	N.22.	01 378 2417
Christmas, C.,	19 Hawthorne Gardens,	N.21.	01 276 7716
Christmas, D.J.,	1 Patton's Way,	N.11.	01 414 4003
Christmas, L.,	236 Pontefield Road,	N.9.	01 368 2164
Christmas, G.K.,	5 Ascot Avenue,	E.4.	01 427 5321
Christmas, N.,	29 White Bear Lane,	E.11.	01 386 6845

   Remember that where surnames are the same it is the initials which are used for alphabetical arrangement in the telephone directory.

   Answer each of the following questions in a sentence.

   a) Whose telephone number is 01 368 2164?
   b) Who lives at Patton's Way, N.11?
   c) What is Mr N. Christmas's telephone number?
   d) Which two Mr Christmases have a telephone number ending with the same figure?
   e) What is the address for the number 01 369 0122?

3. The names of the 'Christmases' in the telephone directory shown have not been put in the correct order. Re-write the whole section putting every name in the correct order.

4. Look at this map and then answer the questions in as few words as possible.

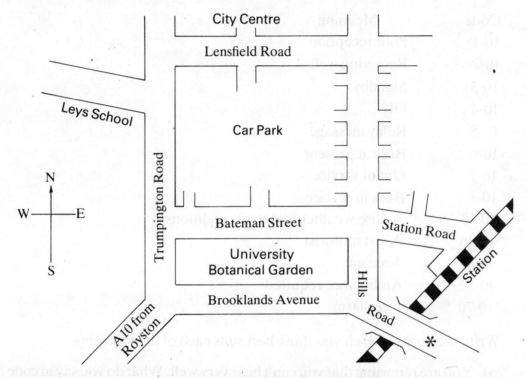

a) What street forms the northern boundary of University Botanical Garden?
b) What is the number of the road which Trumpington Road leads into when going south?
c) What is the road called which leads to the station?
d) If you wanted to go from Trumpington Road to Hills Road, and pass the southern boundary of the Botanical Garden, where would you walk?
e) Which road is immediately north of the car park?
f) Name all the roads which border the Botanical Garden.
g) Note where * is marked on the map. Imagine you have to walk from this point to Leys School, passing the eastern and northern boundaries of the Botanical Garden as you do so. Describe your route and don't forget to name the roads and streets and when and where you would turn.

Test 8

1. The following is a system of numbers used when speaking in radio communication. These numbers were originally taken from the FBI Manual, but TV, films and books have now made them well known.

Code	Meaning
10-1	Poor reception
10-2	Receiving well
10-3	Standby
10-4	OK
10-5	Relay message
10-6	Busy at present
10-7	Out of service
10-8	Back in service
10-13	Advise weather and road conditions
10-46	Assist motorist
10-50	Accident
10-52	Ambulance required
10-70	Fire alarm

   Write the answer which you think best suits each of the following:

   a) You are reporting that you can't hear very well. What do you say in code?
   b) You are preparing a message which you haven't quite got ready. What code do you use?
   c) Something important is taking up your time and you can't receive a message at the moment. What do you say in code?
   d) Your radio has been temporarily out of order. What is your coded message when it is repaired?
   e) You receive a message saying 10-13. What does the questioner want to know?
   f) You have received and understood a message. What do you say in code?
   g) By what code message would HQ tell you to go to the help of a stranded motorist?
   h) What coded message would you send first to report an accident?

2. Here is an example of a simple code:

   THE CODE WORD FOR TODAY IS BLUE

   (printed upside down and reversed)

18

a) Decode the sentence and write it out in full.
b) How is the word TODAY written in this code?
c) Write ESPIONAGE in this code.
d) How many *letters* do you have to change in decoding the word: YRTNUOC?
e) How many *letters* stay the same in decoding: DETALOSI?
f) Write this sentence in the code: BEWARE OF THE SPY IN BLACK.

3. Look at these words: latest – last;   selected – seed.

   Notice how the second word in each case is formed from some of the letters of the first word. Now write a second word for each of the following:

   a) received b) several c) Hertfordshire
   d) divided   e) libraries e) f) wishing

4.
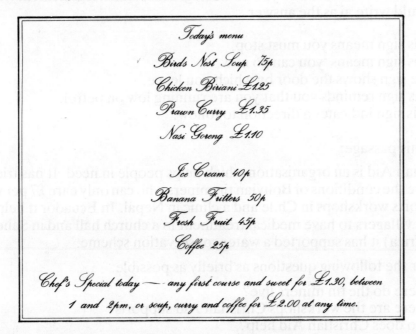

Today's menu
Birds Nest Soup   75p
Chicken Biriani   £1.25
Prawn Curry   £1.35
Nasi Goreng   £1.10

Ice Cream   40p
Banana Fritters   50p
Fresh Fruit   45p
Coffee   25p

Chef's Special today — any first course and sweet for £1.30, between 1 and 2pm, or soup, curry and coffee for £2.00 at any time.

Answer each of the following questions in a sentence.

a) Which is the most expensive dish on the menu?
b) How many soups are there to choose from?
c) Which is the least expensive sweet?
d) Why is the 'Chef's Special' good value?
e) Could you get the 'Chef's Special' at 1.55pm?
f) Could you have the 'soup, curry and coffee' at 12 noon, 1.15pm or 2pm?
g) Apart from soup, how many drinks are on the menu?

5. Here are twelve methods of transport:

   bulldozer   aeroplane   bicycle   barge   scooter   horse
   helicopter tractor   tank   camel   car   canoe

   Pair each one with the other in the group that is most similar to it.

19

Test 9
(*You need a ruler marked in cms. for this test*)

1.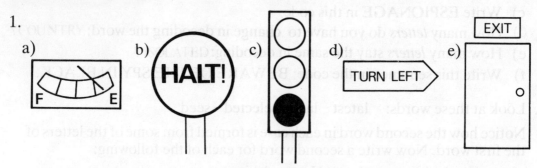

   Look at the diagrams above. Make the correct pairings with the statements which follow. If for instance you think diagram a) matches statement i), then you would write ai as the answer.

   i) This sign means you must stop.
   ii) This sign means 'you can go now.'
   iii) The sign shows the door by which you leave.
   iv) This sign reminds you that you are running low on petrol.
   v) This sign indicates a direction to follow.

2. Read this passage:

   'Christian Aid is an organisation which helps people in need. It has tried to improve the conditions of Bolivian tin miners who can only earn £7 per week; it supports workshops in Chile and a clinic in Nepal. In Ecuador it helps to pay for villagers to have medical treatment in a church hall and in Sahel (W. Africa) it has supported a water conservation scheme.'

   Answer the following questions as briefly as possible:

   a) Where do the tin miners live?
   b) Where are the workshops Christian Aid supports?
   c) Who does Christian Aid help?
   d) Who receives medical treatment in a church hall?
   e) Who pays for the help Ecuador villagers receive?
   f) Where is Sahel?
   g) What does Christian Aid support in Nepal?
   h) What do you think is in short supply in Sahel?
   i) Which of the following would best describe Christian Aid – an organisation which helps Britain; an organisation which helps Asia; an organisation which helps throughout the world.

3. Draw in your book the way in which you think each of these sequences should be finished:

   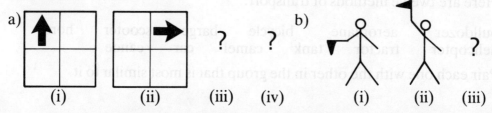

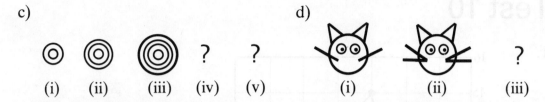

c)   (i)   (ii)   (iii)   (iv)   (v)   d)   (i)   (ii)   (iii)

4. Draw a diagram to illustrate the following instructions.

   Start somewhere in the middle of you page. Draw a line going north for 2 cms. From where you stop, draw a line 4 cms. to the east. From the end of this line head south for 2 cms. From where you have stopped draw a line due west which is 4 cms. in length.

5. Use the picture clues to help you re-write the following passage, putting in the missing words.

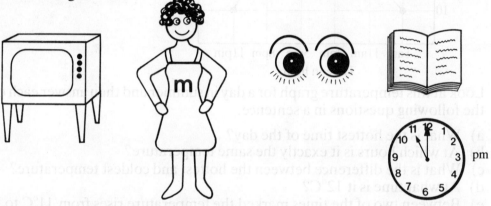

   'Jim liked watching –. His – thought that he watched too much. She said that it was bad for his –. Jim did not agree. He said he learned more from watching – than from reading a –. He said that he never watched late – programmes.'

6. Two words are in the wrong place in each of the following sentences. Write out the sentences putting the words in the right place.

   a) The bark had a loud dog.
   b) Robin Hood was supposed to Sherwood in Forest live.
   c) Julie made a fresh tea of cup.
   d) It was escaped to see how the prisoner had impossible.
   e) When two people duet together it is called a sing.
   f) Most playgrounds have schools.

Test 10

1.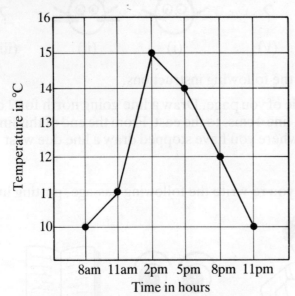

    Look at this temperature graph for a day in summer and then answer each of the following questions in a sentence.

    a) What is the hottest time of the day?
    b) At which hours is it exactly the same temperature?
    c) What is the difference between the hottest and coldest temperature?
    d) At what time is it 12°C?
    e) Between two of the times marked the temperature rises from 11°C to 15°C. Which times are these?
    f) What do you notice about the temperature at 8 am and 11 pm?
    g) After what time does the temperature start to drop?

2. a) If is the last picture in a sequence, in what order do you think the following should be arranged?

    a)   b)   c)   d)

    b) If 3-2 was the final score which of the following scores came first and in what order did the others follow?
    1 – 1   2 – 2   0 – 1   2 – 1

    c) If *night* comes last, in what order do you think the following should be arranged?
    midday   evening   morning   afternoon

    d) If *undeniable* has the most vowels, in what order do you think the following should be arranged, starting with the least?
    station   strapped   appeared   sprung

3. Read this passage carefully:

'It was thick and quite heavy. The edge was as sharp as a razor blade but the end, instead of being pointed, curved as if a thrust in the wind had bent it back. There were flecks of rust where the blade met the handle and there were some chips in the blade itself. The handle was made of bone and it was worn as if many hands had gripped it. Fastened to the top of the handle was a metal ring. This was so that it could be clipped to a belt. John thought it was the best knife he had ever seen.'

There is a great deal of detail in this passage. Now answer each of the following questions in a sentence.

a) The edge of the knife was as sharp as what?
b) Why did the end of the knife look as if it had been thrust in the wind?
c) Where was the knife rusty?
d) What looked to have worn the handle?
e) What was the metal ring for?
f) Was John impressed with the knife?

4. Look at this airline timetable. Answer the following questions as briefly as possible.

Day of Week	Flight Number	Aircraft Type	From	To	Departs at	Arrives at
Mon.	JV 511	DC 10	Gatwick	New York	1400	1600
Tues.	TA 361	DC 10	Luton	Boston	1215	1625
Wed.	JV 433	B 707	Cardiff	Toronto	1405	1750
Thurs.	TA 712	B 707	Gatwick	San Francisco	1200	1530
Fri.	JV 370	DC 8	Manchester	Miami	0900	1600
Sat.	TA 511	DC 10	Gatwick	Chicago	1400	1645
Sat.	JV 423	DC 10	Belfast	Toronto	1115	1325
Sun.	TA 771	B 707	Gatwick	New York	1200	1400

Local times

a) On which day of the week does a B707 fly from Cardiff to Toronto?
b) What time does Flight JV370 land in Miami?
c) Which day of the week has most flights?
d) What is the departure time of the DC10 from Luton to Boston?
e) What type of aircraft makes the Sunday, Gatwick to New York flight?
f) From which airport must you leave to go to San Francisco?
g) You can fly to one city from Belfast. Which is it?
h) What is the flight number of the DC8 from Manchester to Miami?
i) What are the full details of Monday's flight?
j) What type of aircraft do both Saturday's flights use?

Test 11

1.

Type of Call	Charge Rate	Approximate cost of calls for:–			
		1 min	3 mins.	5 mins.	10 mins.
Local calls	Peak	4 cents	8 cents	12 cents	20 cents
	Standard	4 cents	4 cents	8 cents	16 cents
	Cheap	4 cents	4 cents	4 cents	4 cents
Calls up to 56 km. distance	Peak	8 cents	24 cents	40 cents	81 cents
	Standard	8 cents	16 cents	28 cents	56 cents
	Cheap	4 cents	4 cents	8 cents	16 cents
Calls over 56 km. distance	Peak	24 cents	72 cents	1 dollar 21 cents	2 dollars 42 cents
	Standard	16 cents	48 cents	81 cents	1 dollar 61 cents
	Cheap	4 cents	12 cents	20 cents	40 cents

Peak Rate: Monday-Friday 9am-1pm.
Standard Rate: Monday-Friday 8am-9am and 1pm-6pm.
Cheap Rate: Weekends and all other times.

Study the details of these telephone charges and then answer each of the following questions in a sentence.

   a) How long does Peak Rate last?
   b) How much would a 1 min. local call at Standard Rate cost?
   c) What would a 30 km. call for 5 mins. at Standard Rate cost?
   d) How much would a 200 km. call at Peak Rate for 10 mins. cost?
   e) What is the best value of all local calls?
   f) What would a 5 min. weekend call over 100 kms. cost?
   g) How much would an 8.30 am local call on Thursday for 5 mins. cost?

2. Look at this list of questions and answers. Make the correct pairings by matching the right numbers and letters and writing only these down.

   i)   What time is it please?
   ii) Did you enjoy your meal?
   iii) What is the name of that tune?
   iv) How old are you?
   v)   What does the weather forecast say?
   vi) Do you go to the cinema often?

   a) I'm twelve next birthday.
   b) It is half-past two.
   c) Yes, it was very nice.
   d) Never more than once a week.
   e) It is called 'Moonglow.'
   f) We can expect rain.

3. Look at the following diagrams and then write down the number of the correct answer in each case.

   a) If we moved 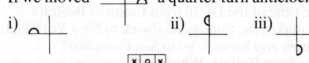 a quarter turn anticlockwise it would look like:

   b) If we completed   it would look like:

c) If we added $2^2 + 2^2 + 2^2$ we would get: i) 12   ii) 6   iii) 16

d) If we moved ⨯ a quarter turn clockwise it would look like:

   i) ┼   ii) ⨯   iii) ⨯

e) If we completed   b a – b   it would look like:
   a – b a
   b a a b

   i) b a b b   ii) b a a b   iii) b a a b
      a b b a   a b b a   a a b a
      b a a b   b a a b   b a a b

f) If we took 10^2 from 10^3 we would get: i) 80   ii) 10   iii) 900

4. Read this passage. It gives some people's opinions about holidays.

   John: 'I like camping holidays. You can get away from other people, climb trees, light fires, play games in the tent. Camping is a great holiday.'

   Mary: 'My favourite holiday is pony trekking. I like getting up early and going to the stables. Then we 'saddle up' and prepare for the day's ride. You get to know your horse really well.'

   Bill: 'I like the seaside. I don't mind where it is as long as it is hot, there is some sand and some sea. Perhaps that is why I am such a good swimmer.'

   Alison: 'The holiday I like best is exploring cities. I find museums very interesting and I like old cities where you can walk round the city walls and look at ancient buildings.'

   Trevor: 'I enjoy staying at home and going out just when and where I want to. When I do this I lie in bed late, and go to bed at night later than I usually do.'

   Each of the following describes one of these people. Write down the name of the person you think is being described.
   a) He is a vigorous person who doesn't mind the weather.
   b) This person probably likes history at school.
   c) This person is a certain kind of animal lover.
   d) This person enjoys being near water.
   e) This person seems less energetic than the rest.
   f) One of these people is an early riser, another is not. Who are these two?
   g) This person enjoys walking.

5. Here are the titles of nine books.

   Blue Star Guide to Italy   The Causes of the First World War
   From Trafalgar to the Present   The Panther Strikes Again
   Plantagenet England   Terror at Midnight
   Murder in Broad Daylight   South America on $10 a day
   Companion to the Pennine Way

   Rearrange them into three groups, and give each group a title.

25

Test 12

1. The following are taken from the key to a box of chocolates:

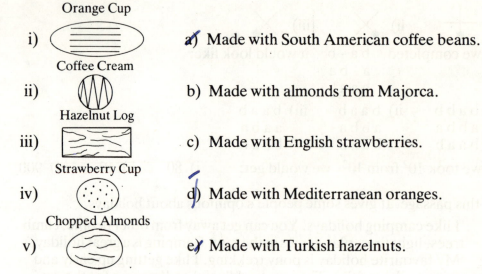

   i) Orange Cup — a) Made with South American coffee beans.
   ii) Coffee Cream — b) Made with almonds from Majorca.
   iii) Hazelnut Log — c) Made with English strawberries.
   iv) Strawberry Cup — d) Made with Mediterranean oranges.
   v) Chopped Almonds — e) Made with Turkish hazelnuts.

   Choose the pairs which match and write down their numbers and letters side by side.

2. Sometimes the size of print on a map shows how big a town is. Example,

   CAPE TOWN — town with over 1,000,000 people
   Nairobi — town with between 500,000 and 1,000,000 people
   Kananga — town with between 100,000 and 500,000 people
   Gaborone — town with less than 100,000 people

   Use this information to help you write down the approximate population of the following towns:

   a) Tabora   b) KINSHASA   c) Lagos   d) Kampala   e) Dar es Salaam

3.

   (a)   (b)   (c)   (d)   (e)   (f)

   John and Joe are brothers. Mary and Tina are the girls with the longest hair. Tina has a brother called Jason. Jason has short, curly hair and, like his sister and Joe, he wears spectacles. Fiona is the quietest child.

   Using the drawings and this information to help you, decide on each child's name. Then write it alongside the letter for each drawing.

4. Here are some well known abbreviations:

   a) BBC   b) C of E   c) DFC   d) FA   e) PE   f) RNLI

   Now pair the abbreviations with the words they stand for. They are all included in the following list.

   Church of England   Football Association   Distinguished Flying Cross
   Royal National Lifeboat Institute   Physical Education
   British Broadcasting Corporation

5. The contents page of a book gives a very brief outline of the subjects which can be found on certain pages. Look at this contents table from a book on festivals.

	Page
Harvest Festival	1
Hallowe'en	28
November 5th	45
Christmas	62
St Valentine's Day	88
April 1st	108
Easter	142
May 1st	153
Midsummer	173
St Swithin's Day	195

   Answer each of the following questions in a sentence.

   a) What page would you turn to if you wanted to find out about the birth of Jesus, presents and Christmas trees?
   b) What page would you turn to for the festival which is listed as being in the eleventh month of the year?
   c) The festivals described on pages 108 and 153 have something in common. What is it?
   d) Which pages would you refer to for information about the two saint's days listed?
   e) Which season of the year do you think page 173 is most concerned with?
   f) The word 'festival' is mentioned only once in the contents list. Which occasion is linked with it?

6. Write out and complete the signs below, filling in the gaps with the correct letters:

   a) __AN__ER!   d) __T__P
   b) SL___   e) E__T__AN__E
   c) __XI__   f) P___V___E

27

Test 13

1. Here are some details of great lakes:

Name	Where	Length (in miles)	Area (in square miles)
Caspian Sea	Asia	680	170,000
Lake Superior	North America	383	31,820
Lake Victoria	Africa	225	26,200
Lake Aral	USSR	265	24,400
Lake Huron	North America	247	23,010
Lake Michigan	North America	321	22,400
Lake Nyasa	Africa	350	14,200
Lake Tanganyika	Africa	420	12,700

Answer each of the following questions in a sentence.

   a) What are the names of the three lakes found in Africa?
   b) Which is the longest of the African lakes?
   c) Only one of these lakes is called a 'sea'. How many square miles is it in size?
   d) The USSR has only one lake listed. What is its name?
   e) Lake Tanganyika is second only to the Caspian Sea in length, but it is the smallest in area. Why do you think this is?

2. If ✓ is the sign for *correct*, ✗ is the sign for *incorrect* and ? is the sign for *can't tell*, write down the best sign for each of the following:

   a)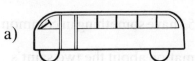
   This is a single decker bus.

   b)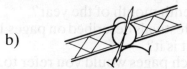
   This is a helicopter.

   c) 4 + 3 = 5 + 2

   d)
   This sausage is hot.

   e)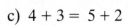
   This is a square

   f)
   This girl's name is Jean.

   g) Labour will win the next General Election.

   h) 1996 will be a Leap Year.

i)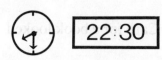

j) $10^2 - 10 = 9^2 + 9$

These clocks tell the same time.

3. A San Fracisco newspaper contained the following advertisement in March, 1860. It was aimed at getting riders for the Pony Express which delivered mail in the American West.

> **WANTED**
> **Young, skinny wiry fellows over 18. Must be expert riders willing to risk death daily. Orphans preferred. Wages $25 per week.**
> Apply: Central Overland Express, Alta Buildings, Montgomery Street.

Each of the sentences on the left below could be joined to one on the right – by using the word *because* to make a longer sentence in each case. Choose the pairs you think go together and write them out as single sentences.

a) Young, skinny riders were preferred.   There was no training given.
b) Applicants had to be expert riders.   It was a very dangerous job.
c) Orphans were preferred.   They had no relations to worry about them.
d) Wages were high.   They were less weight for the horses to carry.

4. Write the correct answer for each of the following as briefly as possible.

   a) If we reversed the order of the months of the year, what would be the fourth month?
   b) If the tenth day of the month is a Wednesday, what is the 25th day of the month?
   c) If Wednesday was the first day of the week, what would the sixth day be?
   d) If Christmas Day is on a Tuesday, on what day will New Year's Day be?
   e) Which is the first month in the year with only 30 days?

5.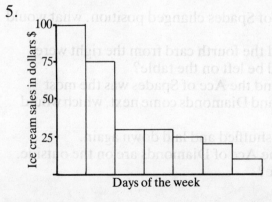

This graph shows ice cream sales for a week. The details were:
Monday $30; Tuesday $30;
Wednesday $25; Thursday $10;
Friday $20; Saturday $100;
Sunday $75.
Redraw the diagram and under each column put which day it represents.

Test 14

1. In a junior school library the Author Catalogue Card for a book looked like this:

   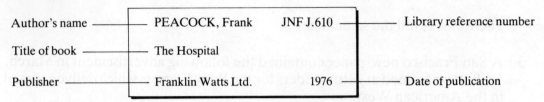

   Draw out, in full, how the Author Catalogue Cards would look for the following two books:

   a) *The First Book of Codes and Cyphers* by Sam and Beryl Epstein. published by Franklin Watts, 1956, JNF J. 652.
   b) *Canal People* by Anthony J Pierce, published by A. and C. Black Ltd, 1978. JNF J. 386.

2. There are 100 pence in one pound (£1.00) and 100 cents in one dollar ($1.00). If £1.00 = $2.00:

   a) How many dollars are there in £10?
   b) How many pounds are there in $100?
   c) How many pence are there in 99 cents?
   d) If a watch costs £25.95 what would it cost in dollars?
   e) If shoes cost $19.00 a pair and you want 3 pairs, how much will it cost in pounds?

3. Look at the four playing card aces below and answer the questions by naming only the cards in each case.

   a) If the cards were collected from the left which would be the last to be picked up?
   b) If the Ace of Hearts and the Ace of Spades changed position, what would the third card from the left be?
   c) If the third card from the left, and the fourth card from the right were picked up, which two cards would be left on the table?
   d) If these cards were given values and the Ace of Spades was the most valuable, and the Aces of Hearts and Diamonds come next, which would be the least valuable card?
   e) Imagine the cards are picked up, shuffled and laid down again. This time the Ace of Clubs and the Ace of Diamonds are on the outside. Which two cards are in the middle?

4. Look at this map.

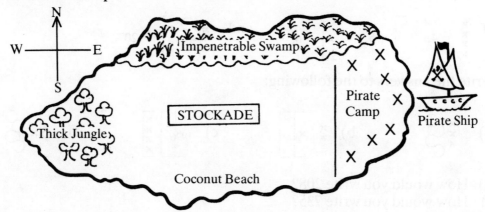

Surinda and Mohammed are trapped in the stockade. Answer each of the following questions in a sentence.

a) If Surinda and Mohammed could escape from Coconut Beach, which coast of the island must they head for? (north, south, east or west).
b) What lies north of the stockade?
c) Would you say that jungle covered the eastern, western or southern part of the island?
d) To put the jungle between themselves and the pirate camp, which coast would Surinda and Mohammed have to travel to?
e) Off which coast of the island does the pirate ship lie?

5. a) If three days ago was the day before Thursday, what day will the day after tomorrow be?
b) If the month after next is June, what was last month?
c) If three years ago it was 1977 and it will be 1986 in six years time, what year is it now?
d) If Rachid is shorter than Hanif and Sadiq is taller than Hanif, who is the shortest?

6. Complete each of the following:

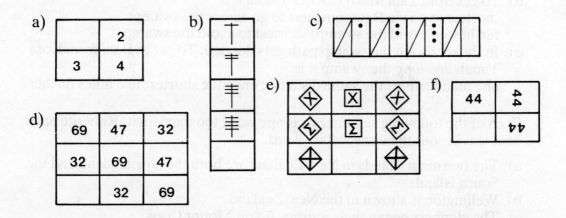

Test 15

1. If ⁞ = 4,] = 5, × = 6, and ⁞×⁞S = 207

   write the answers to the following:

   a) ⁞S   b) ⁞×]   c)]⁞[d) ⁞×S

   e) How would you write 208?
   f) How would you write 735?

2. Each line drawn on the grid below is a path. Note that there is only *one* path across the swamp.

   Answer these questions by choosing the answer you think is correct in each case.

   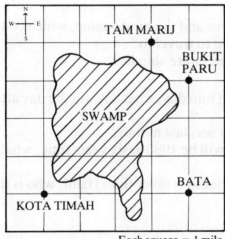

   Each square = 1 mile

   a) The village furthest from the swamp is:
      Tam Marij; Bukit Paru; Bata; Kota Timah.
   b) The distance from Kota Timah to Bukit Paru using the path across the swamp is:
      5 miles; 7 miles; 8 miles; 9 miles.
   c) the village closest to Kota Timah by path is:
      3 miles away; 5 miles away; 6 miles away; 9 miles away.
   d) To get from Tam Marij to Kota Timah it is:
      shortest to go via Bata; quickest to go across the swamp; furthest to avoid the swamp; shortest to avoid the swamp.
   e) In the monsoon the swamp path gets flooded. To get to Bata from Kota Timah *avoiding* the swamp it is:
      one mile further; the same distance; one mile shorter; two miles further.

3. Each of the following sentences has one word too many in it. Re-write each one, leaving out the unnecessary word.

   a) The two main islands in New Zealand are both the North Island and the South Island.
   b) Wellington is a town in the New Zealand.
   c) The climbers began their journey up on Mount Cook.

d) Fruit comes from by Northern New Zealand.
e) Stewart Island is south off of Invercargill.

4. Look at the following and then draw the next two diagrams in each sequence:

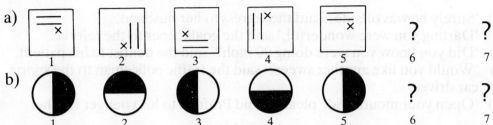

5. The children in a school were asked to fill in a questionnaire which asked, 'What makes a good teacher?' They could choose their answers from the following list:

   a) A good teacher is firm and fair.
   b) A good teacher has a sense of humour.
   c) A good teacher gives interesting lessons which are well organised.
   d) A good teacher is interested in every pupil.
   e) A good teacher is patient and understands the need for careful explanation.

   Each child could make one choice only. When the choices were counted they worked out as follows:

   a) was the most popular choice, having 20 more votes than d). Then followed the other three, with e) being between b) and c). The latter was the least popular choice.

   Write out the list again, putting the most popular choice at the top and working down in order of popularity.

6. These words can be sorted out into three groups. Do this, and then put the heading which you think is right for each group.

   red   banana   giraffe   grape   donkey   yellow   melon   elephant
   brown   pineapple   cow   grapefruit   blue   orange   horse
   goat   green

7. All the children in a group had pets:
   12 had a dog   8 had a rabbit   6 had both a dog and a rabbit.
   a) How many children were in the group?
   b) How many had just rabbits?
   c) How many had dogs but not rabbits?
   d) If two dogs and one rabbit died, how many pets would be left altogether?

Test 16

1. The two parts of these sentences have got mixed up. Re-write them so that they make more sense.

   a) 'Surely he was offside,' said the actress to her husband.
   b) 'Darling you were wonderful,' said the goalkeeper to the referee.
   c) 'Did you know you were doing 90 mph?' said the dentist to his patient.
   d) 'Would you like another sweet?' said the traffic policeman to the sports car driver.
   e) 'Open your mouth wide please,' said Prafulla to his younger brother.

2. Look at this diagram:

   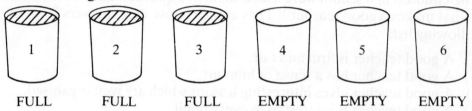

   FULL FULL FULL EMPTY EMPTY EMPTY

   There are six buckets. The first three are full of water. The second three are are empty. By touching only one bucket you can make the bucket pattern look like this:

   FULL   EMPTY   FULL   EMPTY   FULL   EMPTY

   Explain in sentences what you must do.

3. Write down the title which best suits each of the following pictures:

   a) Parachute adventure
   b) Walking in the rain
   c) Arctic adventure

   a) Witches go west
   b) Witches go north
   c) Witches go east

   a) Rainbow Cottage
   b) The house on the hill
   c) Green mountain

   a) Mount Blank
   b) The volcano erupts
   c) Danger

4. 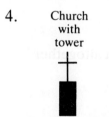 Church with tower    Church with spire    Wireless aerial mast   Site of battle

   The above are symbols for use on maps. Re-write the following passage replacing each group of words in brackets with the right symbol.

We collected the map and started our walk. In the middle of the first field was a (wireless aerial mast). Beyond it we thought we could see a (church with a spire). When we got nearer it proved to be a (church with a tower). After visiting the (church with a tower) we continued over the next field. At the end of it the map said there was the (site of a battle).

5. In each of the following groups write the word which would come *first* and the word which would come *last* if each of the groups were written down in alphabetical order.

   a) Bridgetown   beautiful   Betty   boldness   biscuit   bench
   b) cherry   champion   choose   chill   chasm
   c) dog   dentist   diver   drip   dandelion   dropped
   d) zebra   zither   Zena   Zorba   zeppelin

6. In the index of an encyclopaedia the most important word in a name or title is placed first, which often means changing the order of words in the entry. The first words of each entry are then placed in alphabetical order. For example:

   River Nile, would become – Nile, River because Nile is more important than River
   Lord Louis Mountbatten, would become – Mountbatten, Lord Louis
   Battle of Waterloo, would become – Waterloo, Battle of
   but Solar system stays as Solar system.

   These are then arranged in alphabetical order to become:

   Mountbatten, Lord Louis
   Nile, River
   Solar system
   Waterloo, Battle of

   Re-write the following list in the way you would expect to find it in an index:

   Charlie Chaplin
   Musical instruments
   Lake Placid
   Water sports
   Straits of Magellan
   Liberal Party
   League of Nations
   Cricket
   Jomo Kenyatta
   Bible characters

Test 17

1. The following rules were used for travellers on Wells Fargo stagecoaches:

   > 'Gentlemen must refrain from the use of rough language in the presence of ladies and children.
   >
   > Guns may be kept on your person for use in an emergency. Don't fire for pleasure or shoot wild animals. It scares the horses.
   >
   > In the event of runaway horses remain calm. Leaping from the coach in panic will leave you injured, at the mercy of the elements and hungry coyotes.
   >
   > If ladies are present, gentlemen are urged not to smoke cigars. Their odour is repugnant to the gentle sex. Chewing tobacco is permitted but spit with the wind and not against it.'

   Answer each of the following questions in a sentence.
   a) What is the main reason for the rule that guns should only be fired in an emergency?
   b) What animals are likely to attack anyone who leaps from a runaway coach?
   c) How do you know that children use the coaches?
   d) When would it be in order for a man to smoke a cigar in the coach?
   e) Why do you think tobacco chewers should spit with the wind and not against it?

2. Roman numerals are often used on old buildings and gravestones. To understand them you need to know that:

   I = 1; V = 5; X = 10; L = 50; C = 100.

   The Roman numeral for 4 is IV; 8 is VIII but 9 is IX; 49 is IL and 60 is LX; 99 is IC.

   How would you usually write the following:

   a) XI   b) XIV   c) VI   d) LXX   e) XVIII   f) CL

   Now write these in Roman numerals:

   g) 300   h) 18   i) 101   j) 33

3. Look at these road signs:

On each of the following sketch maps there is a point marked 'X'. Write down the number of the road sign you think would be placed there.

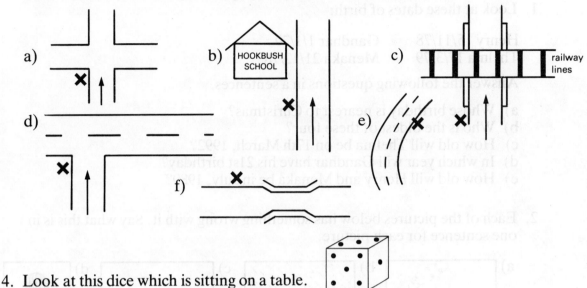

4. Look at this dice which is sitting on a table.

   If you know that opposite sides when added together total 7 (e.g. 5 showing in the front will have 2 on its hidden opposite side) answer the following questions:

   a) What number will be on the side resting on the table?
   b) What will be the total of all sides except the top and bottom?
   c) What is the total of the numbers on the three sides we cannot see?
   d) What is the total of all the numbers on the dice?

5.  Write *True*, *False* or *Don't know* as the answer to each of the following questions.
   a) The men are fishing.
   b) The men are father and son.
   c) The men are brothers.
   d) Eventually they will catch a fish.
   e) They both have fishing rods.
   f) They are having sandwiches for dinner.
   g) They are fishing in a river.
   h) They are standing up.
   i) Their names are Ali and Sunil.
   j) They can both fish at the same time.

Test 18

1. Look at these dates of birth:

   Henry   5/11/78   Gandhar 1/1/79
   Thelma 17/3/79   Menaka 21/12/78

   Answer the following questions in a sentences.

   a) Whose birthday is nearest to Christmas?
   b) Who is the oldest of these four?
   c) How old will Thelma be on 17th March, 1992?
   d) In which year will Gandhar have his 21st birthday?
   e) How old will Henry and Menaka be in July, 1989?

2. Each of the pictures below has something wrong with it. Say what this is in one sentence for each picture.

   a)  b)  c) 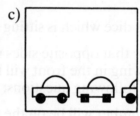 d)

3. Here is a recipe for soda bread.

   Ingredients: 500g plain flour; 4 teaspoons baking powder; 1 teaspoon salt; 25g margarine; 250ml milk.

   What to do:
   1. Mix flour, baking powder and salt.
   2. Rub in margarine.
   3. Pour milk into a hole in the mixture; move it until a soft dough is formed.
   4. Knead dough on floury surface.
   5. Press into shape, cut a cross on top, bake in a hot oven (220°C or gas mark 7) for 35 to 40 minutes.

   Look at the recipe and then say whether the following statements are correct or incorrect. Write 'C' for those you think are correct. 'I' for those which aren't.

   a) A greater weight of flour than margarine is used.
   b) The salt is used in the first process.
   c) 38 minutes could be the right amount of time for the bread to be in the oven.
   d) Either a gas or an electric oven could be used for baking the bread.
   e) All together there are five teaspoonsful of ingredients.
   f) The milk helps the mixture to be turned into a soft dough.
   g) The margarine is used after the bread is made.
   h) The milk used must be hot.

4. Some words have more than one meaning, although the sentence they are in usually shows which meaning applies. For example,

   The boy threw a six with the die.
   i) die – to lose life
   ii) die – a small cube with numbered sides.
   The 'die' used in this sentence is the one whose meaning is described in ii).

   Answer the following by writing the number of the definition which fits each sentence.

   a) Philip was cosy in bed.
      i) cosy – snug, comfortable
      ii) cosy – covering to keep a teapot warm
   b) When mum was in a good mood she often called Garfield 'honey.'
      i) honey – a sweet, thick fluid
      ii) honey – an affectionate name for somebody
   c) A row of soldiers stood to attention.
      i) row – to move a boat with oars
      ii) row – a line of persons or things
   d) There was a scene in the shop when the customer had to wait for half an hour.
      i) scene – place of action in a play
      ii) scene – episode in a play.
      iii) scene – a view
      iv) scene – an unpleasant display of bad temper.
   e) The fisherman looked with concern at the approaching wave.
      i) wave – a ridge on the sea's surface.
      ii) wave – a unit of disturbance of sight or sound.
      iii) wave – a curve in the hair.
      iv) wave – a signal given with an arm.

5. If 1000 metres = 1 kilometre, and 8 kilometres = 5 miles:

   a) How many metres are there in 5½ kilometres?
   b) How many kilometres are there in 75,500 metres?
   c) How many kilometres are there in 10 miles?
   d) How many miles are there in 20 kilometres?
   e) How many metres are there in 15 miles?

6. One four letter word will complete each of the four words in the following groups. What is it in each case?

   a) ....card   b) ....erina   c) ....watch   d) ....acle
      ....man   ....et   ....ped   ....ative
      ....age   ....ad   ....per   ....peg
      ....er   ....oon   ....page   ....h

Test 19

1.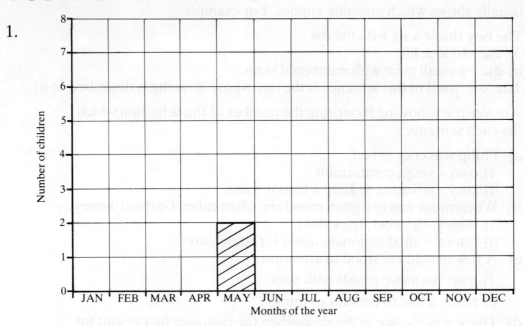

    Look at this graph. It shows that two children in a class have their birthdays in May. The other birthdays are as follows:

January	– 4 children	August	– 1 child
February	– 5 children	September	– 1 child
March	– 3 children	October	– 2 children
April	– 4 children	November	– 1 child
June	– 3 children	December	– 3 children
July	– 8 children		

    Copy the graph out and complete the rest of it using the information given.

2. Here is the Contents page from a magazine:

    ### HOW CONTENTS

Features	Page	**Fiction**	Page
How's successful year	2	Danger in Damascus by Joel King	3
With a dog in the desert	11	Caribbean Carnival by Lara John	38
An interview with Miss World	18	African Holiday by Eli Nboto – Episode 4	19
Leisure		**Do it yourself**	
Book reviews	58	Change your spark plugs	25
Film reviews	59	Getting the best from a window box	27
This month's best buys	60		
Fashion		**Health**	
Jackets for 'him & her'	30	Slim – but be careful	40
Make your own pullover	34	Walking is good for you	43
Hats of the last century	37	Your tear out exercise chart	46-57
Recipes for the month			
A variety of long, cool drinks	29		

Answer the following questions in sentences.

a) Which pages does the magazine invite you to tear out?
b) Which page would you turn to to read about films?
c) How many interviews does the magazine contain?
d) Would you say this was a weekly, monthly or quarterly magazine?
e) Which section would you turn to for help with your car?
f) What exercise does the magazine say is good for you?
g) How many years of hats are discussed in the fashion section?
h) Which episode of *African Holiday* would you expect to have been in the last issue of **How**?

3. Use the graph in Question 1 to answer the following as briefly as possible.

a) In which month were the most children born?
b) How many months had three children born in them?
c) Were more children born in the first half of the year or the second half?

4. Write down which you think is the most likely of the two descriptions for each of the following pictures:

a)
This hand is picking up dynamite.
This hand is reaching for a drink.

b)
This girl is throwing something away.
This girl is receiving a present.

c)
Here is a car parking.
This car is in a hurry.

d)
This boy has had a letter saying he has won a holiday.
This boy has just received his next dental appointment.

e) 'Strongarm attacks'
'Arms and the Man.'

5. a) If ADBC means RUST what does CADBC mean?
b) If ZYXWVU means MAKING what does XWVU mean?
c) If LXYZQRSCBTR means PANDEMONIUM what does RQZBTR mean?
d) If PQRSTUS means SHORTER what does QRSPU mean?
e) If FGHI means MALE what does HGFI mean?

Test 20

1. Read this poem and then answer the questions below.

   Problems Page
   Dear Maureen,
   I am a lamp post.
   Every Saturday at five o'clock
   three boys
   wearing blue and white scarves
   blue and white hats
   waving their arms in the air
   and shouting,
   come my way.
   Sometimes they kick me.
   Sometimes they kiss me.
   What shall I do
   to get them to make up their minds?
   Yours bewilderedly,
   Annie Onlight.   *by Michael Rosen*

   a) Is this poem about
      a lady   friends meeting   football fans and a lamp post?
   b) When the fans are celebrating do they
      kick the lamp post   kiss the lamp post   ignore the lamp post?
   c) What are the colours of the fans' team
      red and white   black and yellow   green   blue and white?
   d) Which of the following words best describes the fans at 5 pm on a Saturday
      calm   orderly   boisterous   peaceful?
   e) *Annie Onlight.* Look at this name carefully. Can you think of a way of spelling it so that it describes something seen on streets?

2. Look at this chart of oven temperatures and then answer each of the questions in a sentence.

Electric oven°F	*Gas oven marks*	*Description*
250	½	lukewarm
275	1	cool
300	2	cool
325	3	medium
350	4	medium
375	5	moderately hot
400	6	moderately hot
425	7	hot
450	8	hot
475	9	very hot

a) Which two electric oven temperatures are classed as *moderately hot*?
b) What gas mark is the same as 425°F?
c) By how many degrees Fahrenheit is gas mark 6 hotter than gas mark 3?
d) Between which two temperatures, in degrees Fahrenheit, would you put a dish which had to be cooked in a *hot* oven?
e) According to this chart which is warmer – lukewarm or cool?

3. Complete the following in your book:

a)
| Aa | Bb |
| Cc | |

b)
| 4 | 8 |
| 12 | |

c)
abc	bcd	cde
def	efg	fgh
ghi		

d)
✗	✗	✳
✳	✗	✗
✗		✗

e)
1	21	321
		4321

f)
●	○	◍
◍	●	
○	◍	

4. In a school a vote was taken to show which were the children's favourite colours. The children voted like this:
red 65, yellow 70, blue 53, green 86, purple 74, brown 70, black 48

a) Make a list of the colours, putting the highest scoring first and working down.
b) Arrange the colours in alphabetical order, putting the number of votes they got beside each.

5. Complete this diagram using the information given in question 4.

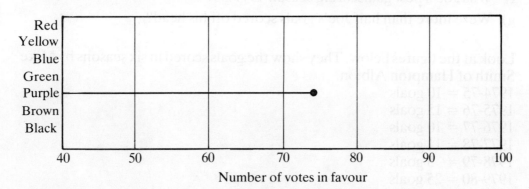

6. Read this passage carefully. When you have done so, write it out filling in the blank spaces with words chosen from the following group:

funny   happiest   cinema   horses   kinds

One of the children's favourite outings was a visit to the —.
They liked different — of films. Anthony liked films about animals, particularly —. The twins enjoyed laughing so they liked — films. When dad went he was — when the programme contained an adventure film.

43

Test 21

1.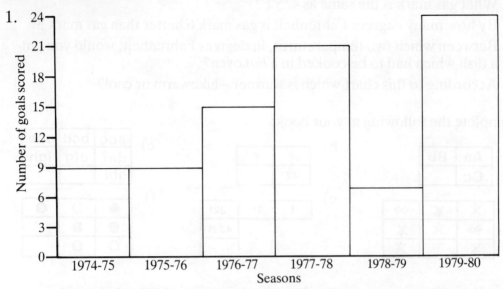

   The graph above shows the goal scoring record of Joe Wilson, Melchester Rover's centre forward. It covers six seasons. Using the information given, answer the following questions by writing: *Yes*, *No* or *Not Known*.
   a) Did Joe score the same number of goals in two consecutive seasons?
   b) Was his best season in 1976-77?
   c) Did Joe break his leg in season 1978-79?
   d) Was Joe capped for England in 1979?
   e) Did Joe's goalscoring improve during the first four seasons?
   f) Was Joe's best goalscoring season 1979-80?
   g) Were more than half Joe's goals scored off his head?

2. Look at the figures below. They show the goals scored in six seasons by Mike Smith of Hampton Albion.
   1974-75 = 10 goals
   1975-76 = 15 goals
   1976-77 = 10 goals
   1977-78 = 11 goals
   1978-79 = 5 goals
   1979-80 = 25 goals
   Now draw a graph to show this goalscoring record.

3. A theatre company visited six African towns. It gave four performances in Nairobi; three each in Mombasa and Luanda; six performances were given in Accra and half as many in Dakar. In Kano the group gave twice as many performances as it did in Nairobi.

   Answer each of the following questions in a sentence.
   a) How many performances were given in Accra?

b) In which town were most performances given?
c) Apart from Mombasa and Luanda, in which other town were three performances given?
d) Which towns had the fewest performances?
e) Were more performances given in Accra than Kano?
f) What was the total number of performances given?

4. Here is a record of a T-shirt order form. There are two mistakes in B which is a summary of the information in A. What are the mistakes?

A

NAME	SIZE	PAID
JOHN	20	1st MAY
SIMONE	20	1st MAY
ELIZABETH	25	3rd MAY
TERRY	21	3rd MAY
JOEL	25	3rd MAY
JASON	21	7th MAY
WAYNE	29	8th MAY
MOHAMMED	29	9th MAY
ALI	25	9th MAY
JUDY	25	9th MAY
PETER	25	10th MAY

B

Chest Size	Qty
20"- 22"	4
24"- 26"	4
26"- 28"	
28"- 30"	2
32"	
TOTAL	10

5. John is two years older than Rachid who is a year younger than Lisa. Lisa is three years younger than Maurice.

Answer the following questions briefly.
a) Who is the oldest?
b) Who is the youngest?
c) Who is older, Lisa or John?
d) By how much is Maurice older than John?
e) How much younger than Maurice is Rachid?

45

Test 22

1. The following two graphs were drawn to show the weather in the holiday season at various resorts in 1980.

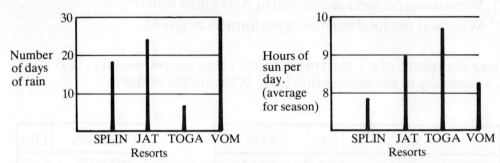

   Read the following statements. By looking at the graphs you can tell if the statement is a *fact* or an *opinion*. Write 'F' or 'O' for each to show which you think it is.

   a) Splin is the coolest place.
   b) For a sunny, dry holiday Toga is best.
   c) Splin could be sunny next season.
   d) Jat has more hours of sun than Vom.
   e) Jat has the second best sun record and the second highest rainfall.

2. The passage which follows is about seven people. From what you are told in the passage, answer the questions by writing down the correct person's name in each case.

   'All the children saw the film. Munsif was amused by it but Rajinder thought that it was boring. Some of the scenes made Shafig furious but Sonia expected them. Petronella was amazed at the acting; Abdul felt rather guilty about the ending and Kamaljit was even quite frightened.'

   a) Who found the film dull?
   b) Who thought it was funny?
   c) Which of the children felt afraid?
   d) Who felt ashamed of one part?
   e) Which of the children felt angry?
   f) Who was most surprised?
   g) Who found some of the scenes just as she had anticipated?

3. Look at this table of facts about football.

Team	Played	Won	Lost	Drawn	Goals for	Goals against	Points
Sunderland	42	30	8	4	101	49	64
Arsenal	42	25	4	13	72	59	63
Liverpool	42	22	10	10	57	32	54
Swansea	42	7	15	20	58	84	34

The teams are arranged in the order of which gained the most points. Write out two more team tables. In a) arrange the teams in the order of which scored the most goals. In b) arrange them in the order of which played the most draws.

4.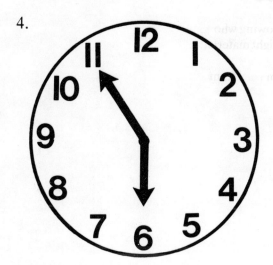

Draw clock faces with the hands in the correct position to show:

a) What time it was 45 minutes ago.
b) What time it will be in 25 minutes time.
c) What time it will be in three and a half hours time.

What would the real time be if:

d) This clock was quarter of an hour fast?
e) This clock was 20 minutes slow?
f) This clock stopped an hour and three quarters ago?

5. Answer each of the following questions in a sentence.
   a) Where would you find the index?
   b) Where is the contents page normally placed?
   c) What would you refer to in order to find a book in a library?
   d) What is the difference between the introduction and the conclusion of a book?
   e) What is the difference between the author and the publisher of a book?

6. a) Rearrange the pictures in this strip so that they are in the right order:

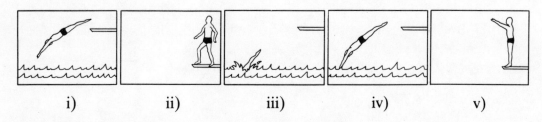

    i)   ii)   iii)   iv)   v)

b) Put the following in order of length starting with the smallest:
   1m   99.8cm   999mm   0.997m   100.1cm

c) Rearrange the following events in the order in which they happened:
   Cook's discovery of New Zealand   Battle of Hastings
   Birth of Christ   Death of Tutankhamen   Second World War

d) Put the following in order of size starting with the largest:
   One hundred thousand 10^2 100×100 1,000 100^3

Acknowledgements

The author and publishers wish to thank the following who have kindly given permission for the use of copyright material:

Andre Deutsch Ltd for the poem 'Dear Maureen . . .' from *Wouldn't You Like to Know* by Michael Rosen.